DON'T FORGET
THE STAR

This Christmas I hope you

DON'T FORGET
THE STAR

*A story of Christmas
through the years of
childhood to parenthood*

George D. Durrant

Bookcraft
Salt Lake City, Utah

Library of Congress Catalog Card Number: 82-72885
ISBN 0-88494-467-0

11th Printing, 1991

Lithographed in the United States of America
PUBLISHERS PRESS
Salt Lake City, Utah

Contents

Johnny wants a pair of skates;
Susy wants a dolly;
Nellie wants a story book—
She thinks dolls are folly.

As for me, my little brain
Isn't very bright;
Choose for me, Old Santa Claus,
What you think is right.

CHAPTER I

I Hope You Don't Get Everything You Want for Christmas

Without bragging too much, I'd say that I was better at making windmills out of Tinker Toys than any other kid in American Fork.

Of course, that might have been because I had so much practice. You see, nearly every Christmas from the time I can first remember such things I'd get a long, round box full of Tinker Toys. I recall one Christmas I wanted a scooter that had pretty good-sized wheels on both ends. You could hold on to a handle that came up on the front. Then you could put one foot on the scooter and put the other one on the ground and push off and away you would go. My friend had gotten one the year before and the two times he had let me ride it I had gone as fast as the wind. I couldn't wait to go lickety-split on that beauty out on the Alpine Road.

You can imagine my disappointment that particular Christmas morning when Santa Claus got confused and, instead of what I'd ordered, he left me another box of Tinker Toys. It was hard to see how he could get scooters and Tinker Toys mixed up, but I guess he has a lot of orders and in those days there weren't any computers to keep things straight.

In an effort to make the best of things, I sat down and pulled the lid off the box and dumped those Tinker Toys out in front of me. In a few minutes I felt a whole lot better, because it's impossible to be unhappy when you are pushing a foot-long little wooden rod into a round hole in a little round wooden wheel. I must have made fifty different Tinker Toy contraptions before Mom told me that my oatmeal was ready. So, in spite of Santa's error, that still turned out to be a fine Christmas.

By the time December was about to roll around again, I'd lost interest in scooters. Remembering the mistake Santa had made the Christmas before, I didn't want to take any chances, so I ordered a little earlier. I did that by telling everybody, including my friends and my brothers and mainly my mom and dad, that I sure did want a Red Ryder BB gun. I mentioned it so often that my brother Kent said that he was sick of hearing about it and told me to shut up. My mother usually got after him for saying "shut up," but for some reason she didn't make a peep that time.

I still can't figure out what went wrong that Christmas. The only good thing was that the box of Tinker Toys was bigger that year and I could make a much fancier windmill out of those rods and little wheels. Besides that, this year those little flat pieces that you put on the ends to make the windmill blades were out of plastic instead of cardboard.

I had a lot of fun that Christmas day. Oh, sure, I'd be lying if I said I didn't feel bad. I still longed for the BB gun. Still, I had no resentment because it's hard to feel that kind of feeling toward somebody as good as Santa Claus. Besides, I knew that I'd get the BB gun the next Christmas.

Eleven months later, just two days before Thanksgiving, I was sitting in my classroom at the Harrington School, which was located just a block north of the downtown stores. We were drawing turkeys and pilgrims and Indians, but my mind was on the BB gun that I knew I'd soon be firing at just about everything in sight. With that thought filling up my mind from one side to the other, I was startled when I heard the 3:30 bell ring. Mom told me that I always had to be home by 4:00. But I couldn't wait to go down to Gamble's store and see if they had the Christmas stuff in yet. With that in mind, I headed south instead of north. About two minutes later I was walking along Main Street. I knew that if I walked faster than usual I could make up the lost time and still arrive home in time to meet Mom's deadline. Besides I wanted to be there in time to hear Terry and the Pirates and Jack Armstrong on the radio.

I hurried east along Main Street. Before I knew it, I was right in front of Gamble's store. I got so close to the window I touched it with my nose. As I was gazing in to try to see the BB gun, I saw something that made me decide I could live forever without Red Ryder's favorite firearm. There in Gamble's window was the fanciest bicycle I'd ever seen. I wish I could describe it. The word *Hiawatha* was printed in gold letters on that fat piece just in front of the seat. It was painted with a color somewhere between purple and red, with white on the tips of each fender. I had never seen anything so beautiful.

From the second I saw it, I started thinking about owning it. I doubt if anyone anytime anywhere ever wanted anything as much as I wanted that bike.

I stood there gazing in that window for a long time. Then I knew I had to head for home. I hardly knew where I was as I walked through the old mill lane. All I could think about was that Santa Claus had to be informed about my desires in such a way that he couldn't possibly get confused. We American

Forkers didn't write any official letters to the North Pole, as far as I can recall. We just figured that if we talked about what we wanted to our friends and to our brothers and sisters and to our fathers and mothers that somehow Santa Claus would get the message.

It was hard to concentrate on Terry and the Pirates that night because I was thinking about that beautiful Hiawatha. It was two days to Thanksgiving. Then I'd have about thirty days to tell everybody I met that I was getting a Hiawatha for Christmas. If I talked about it like that for that many days I just knew that jolly old St. Nicholas would surely get the word. To myself I said, "This year there'll be no mix-up." Then I added, "At least there'd better not be." Having said that, I hit my right fist down on the table to show that I wasn't just kidding around.

I never fell asleep for the next month without having that bike appear in the front part of my mind. I could see myself riding it up the Star Flour Mill hill without even having to get off and push. No kid in the history of American Fork had been able to pedal up that steep hill—I mean clear to the top. In my mind I could see Lelee and Dickie Hampton standing there watching me pedal by. They'd be as jealous of me as I'd been of them when they'd gotten to go to California the summer before. I could see myself riding up north to the canal and then coming back down so fast I'd be nothing more than a purple-red flash.

Finally the long waiting period was nearly over and it was Christmas Eve. It had always been hard for me to sleep on the night before Christmas, but that night falling asleep was as hard as trying to make a snowman in July. Somehow, after what seemed like a couple of hours, I drifted off into the Land of Nod.

It seemed like I'd only been asleep one or two seconds when I woke up. I could hear Dad taking the round metal lids off the stove so that he could put the newspaper and the kindling and the coal in. Hearing that, I knew it must be morning. I jumped out of bed and in the same sweeping motion I pulled on my overall trousers. As I hurried out of my room like a cowboy coming out of chute number one at the Lehi roundup rodeo, I could see the bike in my mind and I knew that Santa had come through. This time he'd kept the record straight. This time the bike would be mine. Without going to the bathroom or even hardly breathing, I hurried through the big kitchen that separated my back bedroom from our parlor.

I was so excited my heart was pounding faster than the motor of a Model A going up American Fork Canyon. I hurried past Dad, who had just struck a match to light the fire, and I entered the door to the room where I knew I'd see my bike near the Christmas tree.

In my haste to cross the room to find the bike, I nearly tripped over the biggest Tinker Toy windmill ever built. I looked straight ahead. There was no bike there. I turned and looked to the right, no bike; to the left, no bike; behind me, no bike.

I stood silently in the shock that comes when *disappointed* is just too weak a word. Then from behind me I heard the voice of my mother. "Look at this," she said excitedly. "Who could have built this?" I looked and she was pointing at the windmill.

My father, who had followed me into the room, spoke up and said, "I got up this morning and came in here and there was old Santa a-workin' on that. I talked to him and he said that he thought George was such a good boy that he wanted to not only give him a bigger-than-ever box of Tinker Toys, but also wanted to personally build him a windmill."

That was quite an honor, and a little bit of a desire to go on living came back into my heart. I walked over closer to the windmill. I'd had a few questions about Santa Claus lately because of what Bobby Jackson had said the week before during recess, but the windmill Santa had built proved that Bobby Jackson was wrong. I couldn't wait to tell the kids at school.

I'd be kidding you if I said I wasn't unhappy about not getting the bike. Yet at the same time I couldn't blame Santa. After all, he had built me a windmill. If he'd done that for every kid, he'd never have even made it out of Utah County that Christmas. I knew I must have been one of his favorites. I couldn't hold any ill will in my heart for him. Besides, I was already looking forward to the next Christmas.

I didn't want to take the windmill apart because of who had built it but I felt he'd be the first to understand if I did. There were a lot more pieces this year, and I built some amazing things.

Two days later I was sitting in my Sunday School class. The teacher was telling us about eternity being a really long time. I kept thinking, "Eternity might be a long time but it can't be as long as the time it takes to get from one Christmas to the next."

My New Year's resolution that year was to get the Hiawatha bike the next Christmas. When I went back to school after the time off for the holidays, Floyd Vest came riding to school on the Hiawatha bike. As I saw that, I started wondering a little about how fair old Santa really was. But then I remembered he'd built me a windmill. I talked to the other kids and he hadn't done that for any of them, so I felt sort of good, at least for a minute or two. But then I'd start thinking that I wished he'd built a windmill for Floyd Vest and then he could have been the lucky one who was Santa's favorite and I could have been riding the Hiawatha. Of course, it didn't matter much because I'd get the bike the next year. But I wondered if Santa knew how hard it was to wait from one Christmas to the next.

Winter was cold that year, spring came late, then the hot summer, finally fall, and then those wonderful days of waiting for Christmas. Slowly it was coming closer. Each day was filled with a little of the pain that always comes with waiting and a lot of the joy that comes from knowing that pretty soon something really good is going to happen.

Santa Claus—
Loving, giving, disappearing.
Here, there, where?
He will be back someday.
Santa Claus.

CHAPTER II

I Hope Losing Santa Made You as Sad as It Did Me

Finally it was just one week—seven days—until Christmas. The 3:30 bell rang and as usual I hurried out of the school and headed north on my journey home. Just before I got to the railroad tracks that ran along the north boundary of the school grounds, my older brother Kent called out from behind me, "Hey, George, hold up." I looked back and stopped and waited as he hurried toward me. Soon he was standing by my side.

We walked along together. For the next few minutes we didn't say a lot because we weren't friends—we were just brothers.

It had snowed a few days earlier, but it was a warm day for December and the sun had been out almost all day. The snow had melted off from the road and water was running along the sides. I liked to put my foot out to stop the little rivers of water and make ponds that would finally run over the tops of my shoes. I could tell I was getting the leather wet and I knew Mom didn't like me to do that, but it was fun and I couldn't help myself.

We'd walked about two blocks without saying anything. Then Kent, who was two years older than I was, spoke. "George," he said in a most serious tone, "look at all the houses on that side of this road." I did as he said and looked to the east side of the road where he was pointing.

He then continued, "That's a lot of houses, isn't it?"

I didn't reply, but I thought to myself, *That is quite a few houses.*

"Now," he said, "look at the houses that we are walking in front of."

I turned my head to the left and saw those houses. "There are a lot of houses along this street, aren't there, George?" he said.

"Yeah," I said, "I guess there are."

"And there are a lot more streets in this town and each one of them has a lot of houses on both sides."

I didn't answer because he hadn't really asked me anything. But I moved my head up and down in agreement because I knew he was right.

I was wondering why he was talking so much about houses but before I could figure it out he spoke again. "George, there are a lot of houses in this town and there are a lot of other towns in America and some of those towns are even bigger than American Fork."

I had almost always believed him because he was older than I was and he'd been to Colorado once. But I had a hard time believing there were towns bigger than American Fork. I'd been to Lehi and Pleasant Grove and both of them together could have fit in American Fork with enough room left over to build a baseball park.

While I was thinking about that, he added, "And besides America there are other countries like New York and Arizona and Europe."

I figured he was right in that because I'd studied geography in Miss Miller's class. I liked geography because I could spell it better than I could spell history or arithmetic. The reason for that was because Miss Miller had said, "Just take the first letters of these words and you can spell geography: George Edwards' old grandmother rode a pig home yesterday." I tried it and it worked. "G—E—O—G—R—A—P—H—Y." It was the biggest word I'd ever learned to spell. That's the reason why I'd pay extra attention when we studied all the places in the world.

Kent still hadn't made his point. "George," he said, "think of all the houses along this street."

I did that.

Then he said, "Now think of all the other streets in town." When he'd given me a little time to think about that he went on, "Now think of all the other towns in America and remember that some are bigger than our town. Now think of all the houses in other countries and add them to all the houses in America."

It was hard to walk along and at the same time think of so many houses. I was concentrating so hard I wasn't even having fun making dams for the water with my shoes.

Kent could see that my mind was chuck-full of houses. He stopped walking and I did too. He reached out and put his hand on my shoulder. Then he said, with the friendliest tone he'd ever used with me, "George, I have a question for you." He looked right at me and I'll never forget what he asked me because it changed my life.

"George, here is my question. How could one man, no matter who he is or how he can fly through the sky, or how many animals he's got pullin' him, in one night go down all the chimneys of all the houses on that side of the street?" He pointed to the east and then while he kept talking he turned and pointed west and said in a louder voice, "And all the chimneys of all the houses on this side of the street?" And then with arms outstretched he added, "And all the chimneys of all the other houses in this town?" He was speaking faster and faster as he said, "And all the chimneys of all the houses in America and all of the houses in all the world and do it all in one night?"

Suddenly and sadly I knew what he was saying. Bobby Jackson had tried to tell me but I wouldn't believe it. Maybe Santa hadn't really been the one who'd built the windmill. Kent smiled because he could tell I understood. I guess he figured he'd filled some kind of obligation. About that time he saw a friend up ahead and he shouted, "Hey, Lelee, hold on." He ran off, leaving me all alone. I walked slowly and I kept looking down at the water on the sidewalk. I knew I'd just lost one of the best friends I'd ever had. I felt like crying. It was almost as if I could hear Santa Claus saying, "Goodbye, George. Thanks for believing in me and thanks for not ever getting mad at me even when you got Tinker Toys. And thanks for being happy even though you didn't get everything you wanted. And most of all thanks for being my friend for as long as you were." Last of all, I thought I heard him say that he'd be back.

Teenage Christmas—
Remembering, disbelieving, longing
Empty, lonely, sad.
Happiness of childhood is behind
and what is ahead?
Teenage Christmas.

CHAPTER III

I Hope You Never Try to Cancel Christmas Because of Sadness

It didn't seem like it took as long for Christmas to come now that Santa Claus had gone away. For the first time in years I went right to sleep on Christmas Eve and I slept in until 5:00 in the morning instead of waking up early as I had always done before.

That year's Tinker Toys were in a bigger box than ever. Even so, the thrill was gone because I knew that not a single piece had ever even been in Idaho, let alone the North Pole. The windmill I made that year didn't seem to turn as easily as those of former years, and it didn't look as much like a real windmill.

The day after Christmas the north wind howled outside and the snow that had fallen a few days earlier was blowing into huge drifts. It was too cold to go outside to play. I stayed in the kitchen by the coal stove. It was the only place in the house where it was warm, except for when we'd build a fire in the parlor stove.

I had just built a drawbridge out of the Tinker Toys. I'd never been able to figure out how to do it before even though I'd tried every year. I was getting so I could figure things out better now that I was older. I took the bridge apart and started to read a comic book. I had left the Tinker Toys on the floor. Mom was busy moving about preparing dinner. She stepped on a Tinker Toy rod and nearly fell. "George," she said, "pick those darned things up before I trip and fall."

When she said that, I silently agreed with her. They were "darned things." It was the first time I'd ever thought of Tinker Toys as being "darned things."

I knelt down on the linoleum floor and began scooping up the pieces. I had always liked the sound of Tinker Toys dropping into the box.

I soon had all the pieces in their round home. I walked to the side of the stove, reached up, and put the box on the shelf that was connected to the back of the stove up above where the coal was burning.

Mom was making potato soup, stirring it with a big spoon. She reached up for a salt shaker on the shelf where I'd put the Tinker Toys. As she did, she bumped the box and it tipped backward and then forward. Then it fell. As it did, the lid, which I hadn't put on very tight, came off. Nearly every Tinker Toy flew out and plopped into the soup.

Mom shouted excitedly, "George, get a newspaper!" I quickly went to the rack and pulled out last night's *Deseret News* and hurried to her side. As I held it with both hands she started fishing out Tinker Toys with her spoon. In about three minutes she got out what she thought was the last piece. It was then that she finally had time to be a little bit angry. If it had been one of the other kids who'd left those Tinker Toys up there, she would have really been upset. But I was her baby and it was hard for her to get very mad at me.

My dad was better at getting mad and he'd soon have a good reason to use this talent. A half-hour later we were all seated around our table having dinner. Dad was eating his potato soup when a shocked look came onto his face. We all sensed that he had encountered something unusual and we all stared at him. He lifted his finger and thumb to his mouth and pulled out one of the round Tinker Toy pieces that was about as big as one-eighth of a medium-sized potato. He slammed it down beside his plate and asked, "What in tarnation is this?"

Mother, who seemed as scared as a kid who'd broken a window playing ball, explained that a few of the Tinker Toys had accidentally fallen into the soup. Dad was only mad for a little while. Then I noticed he nearly smiled. "Please pass the Tinker Toy soup," he said. He usually wasn't one to compliment Mom on her cooking but he added, "That's just about the tastiest soup I've ever eaten."

That was my last year for Tinker Toys.

Because I was the last child in the family, I think Mom wanted to hold on to my childhood Christmases as much as I did. But that's like trying to reach out to hold on to the water of a river. The next year, a week before Christmas, she met me after school and we went to the back part of the J.C. Penney store to look at the toys. I tried to pretend that I didn't have much enthusiasm for being there. I was afraid my friends would see me there with my mom and ask me what Santa was going to bring me. That was one of the reasons that I quickly agreed with Mom that a magic set would be a good Christmas present for me. She bought it for me while I was standing right there with her. She said that she'd see that Santa would deliver it on Christmas morning. Hearing her say that right in front of the store clerk was as embarrassing as if she'd kissed me.

How can you look forward to Christmas when you know exactly what you are going to see under the tree when you get up on that cold December morning? At the same time, I'll have to admit I did like magicians and I'd always wanted to be one. I was eager to open that box and to start doing magic tricks.

I tried making the coin disappear but I couldn't do it quite right. Mom told me to read the directions again. I did, but I couldn't really understand what they were telling me to do. I hated to admit it, because I was a year older, but I missed my Tinker Toys. They worked just fine without any magic words.

There were a lot of feelings I had on that Christmas day that I didn't tell anyone about because I couldn't really explain them. Along about noon I thought to myself, "Christmas is a dumb day. It's nowheres near as good a day as Thanksgiving. At least you know that turkeys are real and you can count on them to never fly away on you." Besides, I liked the stuffing that Mom made out of bread crumbs. The yams were good, too. Even the cranberries were tolerable on Thanksgiving. But they'd make me queasy if I had to eat them on Christmas.

I started thinking that maybe even Halloween was better than Christmas. My friends and I would pull a lot of pranks on that night and nobody'd get mad at us because they wouldn't know who'd done it.

The Fourth of July was better than Christmas because of the parade, the ice-cold orange soda water, and the fireworks down at the ball park.

The only holiday that I could think of that didn't have Christmas beat was Labor Day. I remembered back to the last Labor Day. I was eating a delicious red watermelon slice with juice running down my chin. Dad said, "Be sure and spit those seeds all around so they'll grow and we'll have more melons next year." I laughed and was happy. It's hard to be sad when you are eating a watermelon. But then out of nowhere a terrible thought came into my mind. I remembered that the next day I had to go back to school. The rest of the day wasn't much fun at all.

As I thought about that, I decided it was all right to be sad on Labor Day because the next day school started, but to be sad on

Christmas didn't make any sense. Thinking that made me all the sadder.

Dad was out feeding the chickens, Mom was in the kitchen cleaning eggs, and Kent had gone to play basketball with his friends. I was all alone, sitting in the parlor by the Christmas tree. Kent had given Dad a little silver metal toy gun for a present as a joke. It shot BBs, but wasn't any threat to the neighborhood birds because it had about as much power as a girl slugging you in the arm. And even with a dead aim you could barely hit the ground.

While I was sitting there feeling bad about feeling bad, I picked up Dad's gun and looked at it.

I shot it a couple of times at the cardboard lid of my magic set box, which was leaning against a chair. Then I looked over at the Christmas tree. I drew dead aim on a blue ornament hanging way out on the end of a branch about halfway up. Of course, I didn't shoot because nobody in all the history of mankind had ever shot a Christmas tree ornament. It just isn't right. It's almost worse than shooting a robin in the springtime.

I lowered the gun and was about to set it aside. The trouble was, I was so sad that I just felt like shooting at something. I raised the gun again, aimed right at the ornament, and slowly squeezed the trigger. It was almost impossible to even hit the tree with that gun, much less the blue ornament, but, incredibly, the ball exploded into hundreds of silver and blue fragments. I was shocked at what I'd done. Then, as luck would have it, Mom entered the room. I've never seen her look more startled. She turned from the mess on the floor and looked at me. I was still holding the gun. There was no use telling her I hadn't done it. Kent wasn't home, so I couldn't blame him.

She didn't get angry. She just looked at me for what seemed like a long time. I didn't want to look back but I knew that I had to. I could tell she couldn't believe that her son George could have done such a thing. I was wishing she'd get mad because I knew you couldn't be both disappointed and mad at the same time. The most painful thing that could ever happen to me was to have my mom disappointed.

I told her I'd pick up the pieces. She didn't say anything, just turned and walked out of the room, her eyes moist. In a few minutes I went in to where she was sitting in her rocking chair. I didn't say I was sorry again because she could always tell how I felt and she knew I was about as sorry as anybody had ever been. She reached out and held my hand. As I stood close to her, I felt that toys didn't matter much. The only thing that counted was not hurting people and doing good things instead of bad things.

Later that day I tried to pick up the pieces of the broken ornament and put them together with glue. I soon knew I couldn't do it, any more than I could put a broken egg back together. I finally gave up and just sat there. I hadn't cried in two years. And I didn't cry then. I wanted to, but I couldn't.

I decided then and there that that would be the last ornament I'd ever break. Just deciding that made me feel better.

I lay down on the floor on my back with my feet close to the base of the Christmas tree. I put my hands under my head for a pillow and looked at all the colorful decorations. I looked up at the star. It seemed more beautiful than it ever had before. As I was lying there, I wished I could go back to the way Christmas used to be. I felt that way because I remembered the happiness of the past, but at that time I didn't know anything about the joy of the future.

Gifts —
Listing, shopping, buying,
Make, bake, wrap.
The best of all are heart to heart
Gifts.

CHAPTER IV

I Hope You Give Some Unbuyable Gifts

The next few years my Christmases weren't anything to rave about. About all I can say for them is that they were better than not having a holiday at all.

Each year my friends and I would still go to the toy departments at Penney's and Chipman's and look at all the new toys. We'd act like we were making fun of the little-kid toys as we'd wind them up and scoot them along the floor. The clerk would say, "Don't play with the toys if you aren't going to buy them." We'd just smile and wait until he was gone. Of course, I knew I wouldn't get anything like that for Christmas because I was too old. Instead I'd just get a bunch of new clothes like socks and scarves and a coat and a toboggan hat and mittens. That excited me about as much as learning that the dessert at supper was going to be rice pudding with raisins.

The years went by slowly, but they still went by, and finally I was fifteen. That Christmas I told Mom what I wanted. I seemed to have more luck with her than I had had in the past with Santa. She followed my desires and I got a navy blue sweater that you'd pull over your head instead of buttoning. It was just like the one that Walter Bowen got from his uncle who went in the Navy. I also got a white sports coat. I put on that sweater and the white coat. There wasn't a speck of dirt on me and I looked pretty good. I couldn't wait for school to start so I could show up at the basketball game with Pleasant Grove in those clothes. If Louise saw me dressed like that, she'd really be impressed. Those clothes made that Christmas better than it had been since the end of the Tinker Toy days. It moved ahead of Halloween and the Fourth of July on my list of favorite holidays. But Thanksgiving was still number one with me.

When I was sixteen, Christmas made a bid to challenge Thanksgiving. That was the year Delmar Fraughton, my best friend, told me about mistletoe. But I must have stood under a sprig for two hours at the ward Christmas party, and all it did was keep the girls on the other side of the cultural hall. Thanksgiving stayed at the top of my list of favorite holidays.

Finally, I became a senior in high school. This was the year in which I was sure that all my dreams would come true. This was the year when I'd grow tall. This was the year when the girls would officially discover me. This was the year when I'd be student-body president. This was the year I'd be a bona fide basketball star for the American Fork High Cavemen.

But things were working out for me about like the presidential election worked out for Dewey. I didn't grow tall like I wanted. I still didn't dare put my arm around a girl and walk her down the hall. I wasn't a student-body officer. It was four days before Christmas and we'd already played six preseason basketball games—and I sure wasn't a star because it's hard to be a star if you're sitting on the bench. It seemed like none of my dreams was going to come true. I tried to be happy and I acted like I was happy and a lot of the time I was happy. But there was a deep corner of my heart that was hurting.

That night in practice I'd missed a couple of easy shots and the coach looked at me and shouted, "George, what's the matter with you?" When a coach asks that, it's almost as bad as having a girl laugh when you ask her to go to the junior prom. In the locker room after practice all the other guys were shouting. Delbert Hoaglund yelled, "We'll beat Lehi so far they'll all want to drown themselves in Utah Lake." But I wasn't saying anything because I knew that after what the coach had said I'd be watching the game from the bench.

Without even showering, I quickly dressed and headed out the side door of the gym into the cold December air. Over and over in my mind I could hear the words, "George, what's the matter with you?" I tried to answer that question to myself but I couldn't. It seemed like there was nothing really wrong except that everything was sort of wrong. It was dark already even though it was only 5:30. The snow was about six inches deep with a thick crust, and in most places I could walk on top of it without falling through.

I pulled my toboggan hat down over my ears and put my hands in the pockets of my plaid woolen coat. I walked as fast as I could. I crossed the snow-covered football field. I came to the edge of the school property. I walked up and down the old wooden stairs that the school had built to help us cross the wire fence.

As I headed down the steep hill just south of the Star Flour Mill, I had a fleeting thought that cheered my sad heart a little, and to myself I whispered, "I'll bet Mom will have a good dinner for me!" I don't know what I would have done in those days if it hadn't been for my mom.

Five minutes later with a near-frozen nose I was at the front door that opened right into our large kitchen. Mom was standing by the stove. Hearing the door open, she turned and greeted me with, "George, you must be half-frozen. Take your coat and hat off. We'll soon be ready to eat." She was standing at the stove, and I walked over to get a closer look at the pork chops, or the beefsteak, or the fried chicken. My heart sank as I got closer and discovered that she was cooking potato soup.

I usually tried to be nice to Mom because that's how she always was with me, but sometimes I was more ornery with her than I was with anyone else. I said in disgust, "Ma, why do you cook that stuff?"

"It's good," she replied.

"It's not good to me. You know that I like potatoes and gravy and meat. I practice basketball until I could drop and then I come home and all there is is a bunch of Tinker Toy soup."

"Well, your dad likes it."

"He might like it but I don't. Why don't we ever have what I like?"

"Oh, George, what's wrong with you? Lately it seems like nothing anybody does pleases you."

"Nothing's wrong with me."

Having said that I turned and went to the little washroom that was just through the door in the corner of the kitchen. There were some nails on the wall and I hung my coat and hat on the only two that were empty. I turned on the hot water to wash and warm my hands, and looked in the mirror above the wash basin. My hair had been pressed down by the toboggan hat. That plus my red nose and cheeks made me look discouragingly unhandsome. I pulled my comb out from my back pocket and tried to change things, but I knew it would take more than a comb. One of the things that was wrong with me was the way I looked. As I stood there, I shook my head from side to side with disgust. I don't recall any time when I felt more discouraged.

Mom came over near where I was standing and softly asked, "Guess what?" I didn't reply. She continued, "Your dad went downtown and got a Christmas tree today. He doesn't say much about it but I can tell he's as excited as a little kid. I asked him if he was going to decorate it or if he wanted you to."

Acting uninterested, I started out of the washroom. She stepped aside and I walked past her. I picked up the evening newspaper from off the top of the Singer sewing machine and sat in Dad's chair. I quickly turned to "Little Abner" to see if he'd been caught in the Sadie Hawkins Day race. The way I was feeling I thought Moonbeam McSwine had probably caught him.

Mom went back to stirring the soup. I was reading but I still heard her say, "Dad didn't say it, but I could tell that he wants you to decorate the tree."

"Why me?" I replied. "What's wrong with him? He's the one that bought the tree. I wouldn't care if we didn't even have a tree this year. He's never decorated a tree in his life. Let him do it."

"You know he won't. For years he's loved to watch you kids do it. Now everyone's gone except you. I know that he thinks you'll really want to do it. He even bought two new boxes of icicles and with your artistic talent you could make it very pretty."

"Artistic talent? I'm about as artistic as I am athletic."

"You can do it tonight, George."

"I'm not doin' it tonight."

"Why?"

"'Cause I'm going someplace."

"Oh, George, you don't need to go someplace every night. Why can't you stay home more?"

"'Cause there's nothing to stay home for. It's Christmas time and I'm about as happy as the hunchback of Notre Dame. I want to go to the Owl Inn or somewhere and have some fun." Then I just had a feeling that I needed to blame someone other than me for my problems. So, as I often did, I blamed Mom. With a little bit of unkindness I said in a loud voice, "Besides, why did you ever name me George?"

"What do you mean by that? What's wrong with the name George?"

"George is a dumb name. Why didn't you call me Don like

Afton and Marie wanted you to? If I was called Don, things would be different. Guys named Don get all the breaks. How are you supposed to amount to anything when you have a name like George?"

Mom seemed really shocked by what I was saying. Softly she replied, "George is a wonderful name."

"Not to me it isn't," I said, more determined than ever that my name was the basis for all that was wrong with me. To prove my point I continued, "You ought to hear the guys at school say, 'Hello, George.' The way they say it makes me feel about as bright as a burnt-out Christmas light."

"George, what's wrong with you? George is the best name in the world and it fits you perfectly."

"I know my name fits me perfectly and don't ask me what's wrong with me. I don't know what's wrong with me."

I wasn't reading any more. I was hurting inside and this was the first time I'd had a chance to tell anybody how I felt. I knew my name wasn't the real problem but that was something I could get at and Mom was someone I could say things to without worrying about it.

Dad was out putting the curtains down in the chicken coops. I knew we couldn't eat until he came in.

I started to read again because I had a feeling that all I was doing was upsetting Mom, and besides, what good would talking do?

Mom finished setting the plates on the table. Then she went back over to stir the soup. As she stood there, she looked at me and I looked at her. Oh, how I loved her and I wanted to go close to her and tell her I was sorry. But I didn't. She spoke softly, "George, don't you really like your name?"

I had had enough. I didn't want to say any more. "Yeah, yeah, I like it. Just forget it, will you?"

"Do you know why you're named George?" she asked.

I held up the newspaper and acted like I was reading. I didn't say anything to her, but whenever I was hurting inside I loved to hear her talk. It seemed as if her words weren't as important as the way she longed to make me happy.

She continued, "When I was a young girl, we lived out west of Alpine. There were no houses nearby and so I had no close friends and I was often lonely. My mother was sick and I used to care for her and my father and my little brother Steve. I didn't like living way out there away from everybody. I would go out to the stream to get buckets of water and I'd wish we had water piped into the house. Sometimes I would wish I wasn't so tall. Sometimes I was really unhappy.

"But through those lonely years I had an older brother who was the light of my life. He would often go away to the sheep herd. He'd be gone for weeks at a time. Then finally he would come home, and when he did, he'd always bring me a present. I'd look forward to his coming home more than I'd look forward to Christmas.

"One year, when I was about to graduate from the eighth grade, which was the last grade we had in Alpine, he made a special trip home so that he could be there with me.

"It was in the springtime and I knew the very day that he was coming. I watched for him, and the second I first saw him at the other end of the long road that led to our house, I ran to meet him. He got off his horse and gave me a hug and lifted me right off my feet.

"The first thing he said was, 'Marinda, I hear you're about to graduate. I'm proud of you. I was thinking you'd need a new dress to graduate in.' He then reached into his pocket and pulled out a gold piece. I'll always remember him handing it to me and smiling. It was one of the happiest moments of my life.

"Several years went by and I married your father. We had eight children before you were born. Just two months before you were to come into the world my dear brother, still a young man, suddenly died. I was heartbroken and wondered if I could ever quit crying. In my prayers I told Heavenly Father that if you were a boy I'd name you after him."

Tears filled Mother's eyes. As I looked at her, she was hardly able to speak as she said, "His name was George." I'll never forget the way she said that name. I'd never heard it that way before. She wiped her eyes with her apron and her gray hair seemed to shine as she added, "That's why when you were born I named you George. To me the name George is the grandest name of all."

I don't know what it was about that story. Maybe it was just the way Mom told it. Maybe it was that I needed something special, or maybe it was just that it was so near Christmas. Whatever it was, I suddenly felt different inside. Mom wiped the tears from her eyes with her yellow apron and hurried to finish preparing dinner before Dad came in.

To myself I softly said, "George." Somehow it sounded different. I said it again, "George." I sort of smiled and thought, *I like it. It sort of begins and ends the same way.*

As we were waiting for Dad, I got to thinking about how glad I was that Mom's brother George had made her so happy. I got to wishing I could make someone happy. I thought, *The trouble with me is I don't have any gold pieces or any other kind of money.*

About then Dad came in and we all sat down to the Tinker Toy soup. Dad didn't say much but I could tell he was pleased to have such a good meal. I took a big spoonful and as it hit my hungry taste buds I thought, "Mom makes the best Tinker Toy soup in American Fork. It must have extra ingredients." Oh, I'd still rather have had a pork chop and some fried spuds, but I had two bowls of soup anyway.

After dinner I looked in the mirror again and my hair had straightened itself out a little. My cheeks and nose were the right color again. My eyes looked really brown and my nose even seemed shorter. As I combed my hair, I was thinking that, the way I looked, Louise might even accidentally on purpose try to arrive under the mistletoe at approximately the same time as I did.

Outside I could hear a car honk three times. I knew it was Lum Nelson in his dad's '41 Chevrolet.

I opened the door and bounded down the three porch steps in a single leap. As I ran toward the front gate, I almost slipped on the ice-covered walk.

From behind me I heard Mom shout, "George, if you have to go, come back and get your coat."

A few seconds later I was back at the front door and then in the kitchen. Mom was doing the dishes. When I came in, she looked around and was startled to see me. "I thought you were going out for the night."

I smiled and replied, "I was but I changed my mind." Dad was sitting in his rocking chair reading the front page of the newspaper. I walked over and sat on the part of the stove called the reservoir, which is where the water used to be heated before we got the hot-water tank. It was warm there and it was a great place to sit on a cold night. Dad was not more than six feet away, so I could talk softly and he could still hear me. "Dad," I said, "I was thinking I'd like to decorate the tree you got. Mom said you even bought two new boxes of icicles. That ought to make our tree the best one in town."

Dad lowered the paper and looked at me. He didn't say anything but as he lifted the paper up again I thought I even saw him smile a little bit.

I jumped down from my warm seat and asked Mom if the decorations were in the box above the closet in the back bedroom. She said they were and in a minute I had them. Dad had already put a wooden stand on the tree and it was in the parlor just waiting to be decorated. I stood in the doorway that separated the kitchen from the parlor and before closing the door I said, "Don't you two come in here until she's all decorated."

I looked through our phonograph records until I found the one with "Silent Night" on one side and "O Little Town of Bethlehem" on the other. I found the crank and wound the Victrola up as tight as she'd go. I didn't want to have to wind her again until I'd finished my special mission.

Hanging two boxes of icicles on a tree takes a lot of time, especially if you are hanging each of them just right so that it dangles down straight for a foot or so. I wasn't in any hurry because I was about as happy as I'd been in years and I was singing, "Silent night, holy night." I sounded good enough to give Bing Crosby a scare. Every once in a while I'd softly say the name "George."

Finally the tree was nearly all decorated. I'd just moved a red ornament to where a blue one had been and the blue one to where the red one had been. I was standing back near the opposite wall so I could get a good look at the balance of my artistic labors. I was thinking so hard about what to do next that I was startled to hear my mom say, "George, your dad and I wondered why it's taking you so long." Then she saw the tree. "Oh, George, it's beautiful!" I was thrilled at how happy she looked. I loved it when I made her happy.

Excitedly I said, "I'll plug in the lights and she'll look even better." I crouched down and pushed the plug in. As I walked over to be near Mom and Dad, I could see the red and blue reflections in Dad's dark brown eyes. He didn't say anything but I could tell that he felt better than he would've if I'd just given him a gold piece. I'd never seen him look happier. I felt like a real George.

We all three stood there for a few seconds with the kind of feelings that you have when you are with your family and you're happy. Then Dad in his low and slow voice said something that I will never forget: "George, don't forget the star." I looked up at the top of the tree. Sure enough, I had forgotten it. I laughed and said, "How could I forget that?" I walked quickly to the bench, picked it up, stood on a wooden chair, and gently placed the star on top of the tree. Dad didn't speak but, as I looked over at him, he nodded his approval.

Usually one story from a mother to a troubled son doesn't change things as dramatically as I have portrayed. But many stories and words of love from a mother or a father to a child can over time bring about a miracle.

I don't remember what presents I bought for Mom and Dad that year. They couldn't have been much, for as I said I had little money. But I'll never forget that night when I stayed home and decorated the tree. I'll never forget that night when I made my mom and dad happy by giving them that unbuyable gift—the gift of myself.

I don't remember in much detail many of my teenage Christmases, but I remember that one because it was that Christmas that I began to dream not of what I could get but rather of what I could give.

Seldom is a war won in a single skirmish. Since that Christmas I have continually struggled against selfish desires. I continually try to answer in my own soul the questions of who I really am and what I can really give. But on that Christmas the seeds were planted that through the years would grow to the point where I could more fully give the gifts of my heart and in so doing follow Dad's words, "Don't forget the star."

They looked up and saw a star
Shining in the East beyond them far,
And to the earth it gave great light,
And so it continued both day and night.

CHAPTER V

I Hope Your Christmas
Really Becomes Christmas

If on one particular day many years ago you had asked me, "George, what kind of Christmas are you going to have?" I don't think I could have answered without breaking into tears.

You see, that was the first time in my life that I had been away from home at Christmastime. And when you are your mother's baby like I was, being away from her and your family for the first time at Christmas is more than you or any person should ever have to endure.

In mid-November of that year, I had left the New York harbor aboard the great ship *Maritania*, bound for a two-year mission in the British Isles. After a seasick week I arrived in Southhampton, England. I spent a few busy and eventful days in London, and then received my specific assignment. Now, as

Christmas approached, I was in a city called Kingston Upon Hull. The excitement of travel had worn off and had gradually and completely been replaced by discouragement. I'd been in Hull, as it was called, just one month and I had been homesick since I'd arrived. As day by day and hour by hour Christmas came closer, that most painful malady of the heart grew ever worse.

To add to my woes, the cold damp foggy air filled my lungs as, with my companion, I pedaled my bicycle for miles to call upon those who would listen to messages of the restored gospel. Under such conditions my nose began to run on December the twenty-second. I began to cough on the twenty-third, and on Christmas Eve I had an almost perfect cold.

As soon as I had arrived at my assigned area, I had written home:

> Dear Mother,
> My address is Elder George Durrant, 4 The Paddock, Anlaby Park, Hull, England. Please let all the family and all of my friends know that if they and you desire to send me Christmas cards and gifts they can send them to that address. Please call as many people and advise them of this as quickly as you can.

I hopefully supposed that this letter would get home in time for the returning mails to bring me some measure of Christmas joy.

Each day I'd wait almost breathlessly for the postman. He'd be laden with so many cards and gifts that instead of trying to slide them through the mail slot in our front door he would bang the brass door knocker. I'd throw the door wide and reach out and grab the entire pile. Surely at least one-half of these would be mine. With trembling hand I'd pull one from the pile and read. The first one was addressed, "Elder Tagg." The next one, "Elder Tagg." The third, "Elder Tagg." One after another the same name appeared. I was soon willing to settle for just one. But there wasn't one. In all, during the week before Christmas Elder Tagg received thirty cards and several gifts. As he'd open each card, I'd have to look away.

Finally, it was the last mail delivery day before Christmas. I had prayed fervently that I'd receive some Christmas greeting from home. The mailman came up the walk. The door knocker clanged. He reached out and so did I. To my joy there were seven cards and a small brown package. One by one I read the addresses and handed the first, the second, and finally all of the cards to Elder Tagg and then I tossed him the present. I could tell that he was deeply sorry and I knew that if he could have he would have given me any one or even all of the cards and the gift.

I turned away and ran up the stairs to our bedroom. I felt that I needed time to think. As I sat there on the side of my bed, I placed my coupled hands against my bowed head. I wanted desperately to somehow turn the clock and the calendar ahead and just skip Christmas. I knew I could make it through the other 729 days in England but I didn't feel that I had the power to weather this first Christmas.

As I sat in deep silence, the landlady, Nellie Deyes, and Elder Tagg came to the open door. She said, "Elder Durrant, I've come to say good-bye for a few days."

I looked up and she was looking away from me and I could sense that her heart was also heavy. "What do you mean, good-bye?" I asked in surprise.

Without answering she turned and was gone. Elder Tagg spoke softly, "They fear that she has cancer. She wanted to wait until after Christmas to go to the hospital but she just learned this afternoon that a bed has opened up at the hospital and so she must go now."

I was shocked. She reminded me so much of my mother and I'd grown to love her in the month we'd lived in her home.

I went downstairs to where she and her loving husband were just ready to leave for the hospital. I'll forever remember the look in her eyes as she said, "Elder Durrant, I love you. Now you be sure and have a good and happy Christmas." Then she asked if Elder Tagg and I would give her a blessing. Elder Tagg anointed her head with oil. As we both laid our hands upon her head, I poured my heart out to the Lord in prayer that she would soon be well. Later that night she went into surgery. Christmas Eve she died.

When I learned the news, I wanted to pray but I could not. I had had so much love, so much hope, so much faith—and yet she had died. I wondered about many things that foggy Christmas Eve.

Sister Guest, the Relief Society president, had two weeks earlier invited all four of us who served as missionaries in Hull to come at noon on Christmas day for a goose dinner. On Christmas morning at about 11:00 the two other elders came from their home some four miles away to the place where my companion and I lived. The plan was that Elder Tagg and I would proceed on with them to the dinner. We were all greatly saddened by the passing of Sister Deyes but we knew that she would want us to go.

My cold had indeed worsened and the two elders who hadn't seen me for a few days commented on my apparent ill health. After discussing the matter with Elder Tagg we decided that I shouldn't go out into the damp air. Pop Deyes was at home and I said I'd stay with him. The others agreed and soon the three of them were gone.

Pop Deyes was in his quarters and wished to be allowed to remain in solitude, so I was left to myself in the front room. It was Christmas day and I was more alone than I'd ever been and more alone than I thought anyone else had ever been.

There were no gifts. There were no cards. There was no Christmas tree. There were no carols. There was nothing. The silence of the room was broken only by the mechanical working of the cuckoo clock. It was now just past eleven o'clock in the morning of the saddest day of my life and it was Christmas.

I moved closer to the fireplace, which was the only source of heat. The glowing embers seemed to be trying to act as my private Christmas lights. Resenting their attempt to brighten my soul, I picked up the nearby metal poker and pushed at each one to crush out its glow.

I lowered my head and cradled it in my left hand. I sat that way until a "cuckoo" brought me back from where I had been. It was noon.

The room was growing colder now. I arose and poured some coal onto the few embers that remained. Now the fire gave off no heat because the new coals had covered the hot ones. I pulled my chair closer to the fireplace. Almost accidentally I looked on the mantel and there I saw my Bible. I stood and reached out and grasped it and sat back down. I really didn't want to read. I was far too sad to read. Yet at the same time, as a new missionary, I needed to know so much. The others knew so much and I seemed to know so little.

It wouldn't hurt to read a little—just a page or two. I opened the book beyond the middle and found my eyes focused on the words, "The gospel according to St. Matthew."

I didn't want to read. I wanted to be home. With clenched fist I hit the open book and then shook my head almost as if I could by saying "no" cancel every painful feeling that filled my sorrowed soul.

Because the pages were right in the line of my sight, I found myself staring at all the words at once. Without a conscious effort I focused on the first verse. I read, "The book of the generation of Jesus Christ, the son of David, the son of Abraham."

Like obedient servants my eyes continued reading the genealogy of Jesus, but my mind was not willing to let the words become thoughts. A few seconds later it was almost as if the words on the page forced my eyes to call my mind to attention. With full concentration I read, "Now the birth of Jesus Christ was on this wise: When as his mother Mary was espoused to Joseph, before they came together, she was found with child of the Holy Ghost."

Placing the fingers of my left hand at the bottom of this sacred verse I looked up at the mantel above the fireplace but I really wasn't looking at all. I wondered, *What does this mean? How did it say it?* I looked back at the page and read again, "She was found with child of the Holy Ghost."

I felt an incredible sense of wonder. Somehow, through a process beyond my intellect, I sensed that what I had just read was among the most important truths ever known. My eyes lifted slightly and I read the entire verse again, this time in an audible whisper, "Now the birth of Jesus Christ was on this wise: When as his mother Mary was espoused to Joseph..." I paused and wondered, *What does espoused mean?* I read on, "... before they came together, she was found with child of the Holy Ghost."

Without looking at the verse I read again from the memory of my mind the words, "... of the Holy Ghost."

I knew I had heard all this before. But somehow I'd never really heard it with my heart.

To my mind my heart whispered, "So Mary is his mother, but Joseph isn't his father."

I noticed a small letter "i" near the words "of the Holy Ghost." I looked at the footnote and read "Luke 1:35." I rapidly turned the pages ahead and eagerly read, "And the angel answered and said unto her, The Holy Ghost shall come upon thee, and the power of the Highest shall overshadow thee: therefore also that holy thing which shall be born of thee shall be called the Son of God."

Letting the book rest in my lap, I touched my chin with my left hand and stared at the coals, which were just now beginning to turn from black to orange. Gently I whispered, "The Son of God." A surge of energy went up and down my spine as I felt my soul fill with light. In a louder voice and with pure knowledge I softly said, "Jesus Christ is the Son of God." That thought caused me to sit more erect.

With half a smile, I turned back the pages to Matthew.

I read on until I came to the words, "... the angel of the Lord appeared unto him in a dream." I wondered, *Are there really angels?* And within my soul I heard the glorious message, "Yes, there are angels."

A few seconds later I was in the midst of my own Christmas pageant. "Now when Jesus was born in Bethlehem of Judea in the days of Herod the king, behold, there came wise men from the east to Jerusalem,

"Saying, Where is he that is born King of the Jews? for we have seen his star in the east, and are come to worship him."

Again I let the book rest in my lap as my mind flooded with memories. I remembered when I had proudly taken the part of a wise man in the Christmas pageant. Because of that memory and the feelings of my heart, my face was now fully covered by a broad smile.

I read on, "...the star, which they saw in the east, went before them, till it came and stood over where the young child was.

"When they saw the star, they rejoiced with exceeding great joy."

As I pictured in my mind that holy star, I could see my mom and dad in the doorway looking in at the newly decorated tree. I could hear Dad's words, "George, don't forget the star." That thought caused me to sit and just stare at the glowing embers. Oh, how I loved my dad and mom—and for a few minutes I was at home with them.

I continued to read, "And when they were come into the house, they saw the young child with Mary his mother, and fell down, and worshipped him: and when they had opened their treasures, they presented unto him gifts; gold, and frankincense, and myrrh."

The fire was now giving off a great warmth but it seemed that the greater fire burned within me. For, in my soul I knew that Jesus Christ was the Son of God, that he had been born in Bethlehem, that a star had shone over where he lay. As I continued to read, I knew that he was baptized in the waters of the Jordan, I knew that he was tempted of the devil but that he overcame all temptation. I knew that he was speaking and challenging me when he said, "Blessed are the pure in heart: for they shall see God." Oh, how I longed to be pure in heart! Of all the goals of life, I could think of none that would be so desirable as to be pure in heart.

As I read every page, paragraph, line, and word of the book of Matthew, I could see and I could feel. As I read of his crucifixion, I remembered the words of the song, "Were you there when they crucified our Lord?" And I was, for as I read I was there and in my heart I trembled. As I read of his resurrection, I rejoiced. My soul was filled with hope as I finally read the last two verses of Matthew. I could almost hear his voice as he spoke directly to me:

"Go ye therefore, and teach all nations, baptizing them in the name of the Father, and of the Son, and of the Holy Ghost:

"Teaching them to observe all things whatsoever I have commanded you: and, lo, I am with you alway, even unto the end of the world. Amen."

Slowly I closed the book and with both hands I held it close to me. To myself I said, "Jesus Christ is the Son of God. There are angels. He did live and teach and love and perform miracles and was cruelly crucified and then he rose again. He is my Savior and this is his Church. I'm one of those he has sent forth. He is with me forever."

As I sat there holding my Bible, it was late on Christmas afternoon. Never had I been so happy in such an inward way. On that glorious day I had found the one who is the heart of Christmas.

I had found him when I felt forgotten by my family and friends. I had found him when I felt the pain of being away from home. I had found him when the death of someone I loved had torn at my heart. I had found him when I felt hopeless. I had found him because I'd followed the star. I had learned what so many have learned, that following the star, and never forgetting, is not always easy. Sometimes the nearer the star takes us to the stable and the garden and the cross, the more difficult the journey becomes.

That Christmas in England I learned that Christmas can be Christmas without a multitude of things. Mistletoe, colored lights, green-boughed trees, yule logs, greeting cards, and Santa Claus each have their own special way of gladdening our senses and delighting our hearts. But Christmas cannot be Christmas without Christ. On that holy day uncontrollable circumstances had pushed all else aside and left me free to follow the star. On that day I learned that Christ does not fit into Christmas. He is not part of Christmas. Jesus Christ is Christmas. In the years since, I've learned that the pressures and selfish desires of life can push themselves between me and him. If I want to "not forget" the star, I must take the time to be alone with him. I must read of him, think of him, and pray to be near him. Then in the east I see the star. I follow it. I find him and when I do I feel free—free to let my soul soar into the realms of the sacred and indescribable joy that I found first in England many Christmases ago.

When the clock is striking twelve,
When I'm fast asleep,
Down the chimney, broad and black,
With your pack you'll creep;
All the stockings you will find
Hanging in a row,
Mine will be the shortest one,
You'll be sure to know.

CHAPTER VI

I Hope Santa Comes Back to You, Because He's Not Just for Kids

After returning from England I hoped that I would never again forget the star. Yet I still longed for the good old days when Santa Claus was at the center of the fun side of Christmas.

Jolly old St. Nicholas had been missing from my life for over fifteen years.

He'd been gone so long that I really didn't know where to even begin to try to find him. I considered contacting Mr. Keen, the tracer of lost persons. When as a young boy I had listened to him on the radio, I had thought he could find anyone. Perhaps he could help me locate my former friend. But I didn't even know how to locate Mr. Keen. Anyway, I sensed that that was not really necessary. I knew that if I was willing I wouldn't really have to find Santa Claus. I knew that if my heart was right, he'd find me.

I realized that to prepare myself for such a happy reunion there were certain requirements that I had to meet, centering around the exciting adventure of having a family of my own.

As I had grown up, I had wanted to be a basketball star, then a great missionary, but never before had I wanted to be anything so intensely as I then desired to be a husband and a father. Having long had such a goal, and with my mission to England now behind me, I was more than willing to enter such a venture. As a matter of fact, I was not only willing, I longed for and dreamed of a little home, a wife, and wall-to-wall children.

I had met Marilyn while she and I served our missions at the same time in England. We had kept all of the mission rules. However, I did have an electrifying handshake. Marilyn had returned home in September and I had arrived back in mid-December. We had seen each other often since my return.

The day before Christmas I borrowed dad's truck and drove to downtown American Fork. I parked and walked toward Garth Reed's jewelry store. I pulled my wallet from my pocket, opened it, and looked at the small number of green bills that were inside. To myself I whispered, "Oh, Santa Claus, how I could use you now! Between the two of us perhaps we can get the size of ring that Marilyn really deserves."

I guess he was busy packing his sleigh, because he was about as much help to me on that occasion as a skeptical banker. Anyway, a few minutes later I walked out of the store with the finest Christmas present I'd ever purchased. As I pulled the truck door shut and pushed on the starter, I said to myself, "If Marilyn accepts this, I'll know that giving is indeed far better than receiving."

That night, Christmas Eve, I borrowed my brother John's car and headed up around the Point of the Mountain and on into Salt Lake City. I went straight to Marilyn's house. I was so excited I could hardly speak and that was all right with her dad because he was watching TV.

We went out to dinner and I was so beside myself that I could hardly taste the meat in my Dee's hamburger. After eating our final french fry we drove up State Street. I stopped the car near the State Capitol Building. As we looked out at the lights of the city, we talked for a few minutes. I couldn't concentrate on anything but the ring. Being with Marilyn was like having a lot of my dreams coming true and a lot more being ready to come true. I was absolutely certain that she deserved the very best and the time seemed right, so I pulled the small box from my pocket and placed it gently into her hand. With observable excitement she opened it and pulled the ring out from the satin slot in which it rested. Then she looked up and over at me. I could tell she was pleased and that the answer was going to be yes.

After a few seconds of silence, while we both looked down at the ring, we lifted our heads and looked deep into each other's eyes. I could see a reflection there. I could see the reflection of the stars of the northern sky. Then suddenly I saw something that I could scarcely believe. There in that amazing reflection I saw, crossing between the stars, some strange sort of vehicle. It was being pulled by several small animals, each of which seemed to have some sort of horns. There in the airborne apparatus was riding someone dressed in red. As far as I could tell, he had a white beard. He was waving right at me and even though he was about two and one-half miles away I could somehow read his lips as he shouted, "George, George, I'm back."

Desiring to see this wondrous sight more directly, I turned quickly, opened the car door, and jumped out. But I was too late. By now whatever it was that I had seen had passed behind a mountain peak and appeared to be headed toward Park City.

Marilyn was surprised at my strange behavior. A minute or two later when I got back in the car, she asked, "What did you see?" Not wishing to appear irrational, I replied, "Oh it was a . . . just a flying saucer." I didn't say anything more to her at the time. I was fearful that if I told her the truth she might think it so strange that she would change her mind about accepting the great gift that by now she had placed snugly on her finger.

Even though I said nothing more at the time, I knew that through Marilyn and the children that I prayed would come, Santa Claus had returned to my life. This time he was bigger and better than he had been before. This time he wouldn't be someone to get things from but instead he would be someone to give things through.

As we drove home that night, I became very silent. Marilyn touched my arm and asked, "What are you thinking about?"

I replied, "I was thinking about all the houses in American Fork and all the houses in Asia and Europe."

She looked at me as if she feared I was not of sound mind. But before she could speak I continued, "Maybe there is a way that he could do it. If he had help, I'll bet he could do it all in one night." Then, after pausing to consider the probabilities, I spoke again, "I know he could, if every father and mother gave him a hand. I'm willing; how about you?"

"Sure," she replied. "Sure." After a few quiet moments she added, "Speaking of houses, I guess you know you passed mine three blocks ago!"

"Of course I know. Santa and I, we know where every house is."

As I made a U-turn, I said, "You know, Marilyn, my brother Kent was wrong. His logic was right about the difficulty of the task but he failed to consider one vital factor." Before I could say more, we were at her house and the time for philosophical discussion was over.

I realize that you may be a bit skeptical about what I really saw in the sky above the State Capitol Building on that Christmas Eve many years ago. I'm sure you would say, "Now, George, we realize that you were too much in love to have really known what you did or didn't see." Then you might continue by saying, "We don't doubt that you saw a reflection, but a reflection isn't reality."

Well, you can believe what you want. But I've got more evidence than one brief sighting to prove my point. I've got twenty-five years of very strong circumstantial evidence. Let's just take one of those years and look at it carefully. You'll have to give up your own Christmas Eve plans and come back in time with me to a December the twenty-fourth when my children were clustered around their early years. Come into my home and just stand back and watch. I guarantee that you'll see things that will remove all your agnostic thoughts about Santa.

You'll see me come home from work and come into the house. The children will come running to greet me because I'm very popular at home. You'll hear Matt shout, "It's Christmas Eve. Santa Claus is coming tonight."

Kathryn will gleefully add, "Yeah, and he is bringing me a Betsy Wetsy doll."

I'll hold Devin on my lap and ask, "What's Santa going to bring you?"

"A garbage truck," Devin will answer with almost uncontrollable joy.

"We'd better hang up our stockings," Marinda will say.

"You're right," I'll answer. "Santa has a lot of good stuff for us. So let's hang up big ones."

Dwight will pull at my hand and say, "Dad, tell Santa to put my stuff all on this chair."

"Okay, and where should he put your things, Warren?"

"Over in this corner," Warren will answer.

"When will Santa get here?" brown-eyed Sarah will ask anxiously.

"Not until we are all in bed asleep," I'll reply.

By now you'll see that I'm so excited I can hardly control myself. Little Mark will say, "I've been a real good boy so I'll get lots of stuff from Santa Claus, won't I, Daddy?"

"You sure will, Markie. You sure will."

Marilyn will say, "It's time for our Christmas pageant. Santa is important, but who is much more important?"

"Jesus," Matt will reply.

"Yeah, Baby Jesus," Kath will add.

Then you'll see a pageant at our house that you'll have to admit is the best you've ever seen.

"Now it's time to go to bed," Marilyn will say with obvious delight.

Soon you'll see the children all dressed in their pajamas. We'll ask you to kneel in prayer with us. We will feel a real closeness as we pause to give our thanks to him who makes family happiness the best happiness of all.

Then you'll watch as the kids head for their rooms.

You can come with me as I go to the bedrooms. "He'll be here soon, Matt, so try to go to sleep," I'll say.

"You didn't give me my kiss," Marinda will call out.

"Mom and I sure do love all of you. We are so glad that Santa is coming. I can't wait until morning. How about you?"

A few hours later the real evidence will be there for you to see. But you'll have to get up early to see it. Don't worry about waking up. I'll wake you because I'll be awake long before daylight.

When morning comes, I'll show you a place to stand near the bottom of the stairs. From there you'll be able to see perfectly.

A few minutes later you'll see the children come down the stairs or the hall. Be sure to look at their eyes. That is where the real evidence is.

Then watch as they move toward the place where the toys are. You'll see Santa as you've never seen him before. But you'll do more than see him in their eyes. You'll feel him in your heart.

The last evidence of all will be to look at me. You'll see a surprise in my expression that will be the conclusive evidence. You'll ask, "George, you seem amazed at what has gone on in this room since we all went to bed last night."

I'll reply, "Of course I'm amazed; aren't you?"

Then you'll just have to admit, "I sure am, I sure am." And you'll know that there is only one conclusion. Somehow, some way, Santa has been there.

The evidence will be overwhelming. You'll know that what I saw up by the Capitol was real. There really is a Santa Claus. A Santa who knows that one of the happiest things we can do at Christmastime is to give something to someone without telling him who gave it. A Santa who long ago volunteered to be the one to take the blame for seven million and sixty-three Christmas mysteries each year. A Santa who agreed that on Christmas morning when parents say, "We didn't give it to you, Santa Claus did," he'll just wink and smile and won't say a thing. A Santa who enjoys getting the blame for things that make Christmas a time for little ones to have a full measure of Christmas joy.

Christmastime—
Partying, shopping, wrapping,
Scurry, hurry, worry.
Stop! Let meaning settle in your heart.
Enjoy some
Christmas time.

CHAPTER VII

I Hope You Have Some Real Christmas Time This Christmastime

Each chapter of life is better than the last one. And the heart of each year's experience is Christmas. It comes a lot more quickly now than it used to. It's no longer an eternity between one Christmas and the next. It seems that nowadays time has been speeded up. Christmases are like airplanes at a busy airport—they are all lined up just waiting to land.

The trouble is that they come so fast and there is so much to do that often at Christmas we are so busy that we don't take the time to have some real Christmas time.

As I think back and try to analyze things, the best part of my Christmases has been those times when I've slowed down and

taken time to just sort of think about things. That kind of thinking and feeling time is best described as *true* Christmas time.

In England on that Christmas Day many years ago, I had
more than a half-day of pure Christmas time—time to read, to
think, to pray, to feel a closeness to him who was born on that
first Christmas.

I had some Christmas time this past Christmas, too.

It was two Saturdays before Christmas. Thanksgiving—my
second favorite holiday—was over and there was a lot of
Christmas in the air.

It was time for the annual Christmas tree purchase. Marilyn
and I don't go together to buy the Christmas tree anymore. I
always want to buy the first tree I see and she can't bear to buy
one until she sees the very last one. Things just didn't work out
and so now she bakes cookies while I go for the tree.

This year I took my young son Mark. As we prepared to
leave the house, Marilyn's last words were, "Don't buy the first
tree you see." That would have been good advice for a less
inspired man than me.

I just felt impressed to go to a certain Christmas tree sales lot.
Once in the lot, I saw thousands and thousands of trees. I stood
silently for a few seconds and then I was impressed to walk
forward, turn right, then left, then back right, then ten paces
ahead, and there it was—the perfect tree. (I wish I could do as
well on used cars.) It seemed to cry out, "I'm the one."

"That's it, Mark," I said.

"It's a good one," he agreed. "But," he added, "Mom said to
look around before we chose one."

"I know she said that but how was she to know we'd find the
perfect one right off?"

By now I was walking to the front of the lot to pay the young
man. "Mighty pretty tree," he said as he nailed it on a wooden
stand.

I thought, "Of course it's pretty. I'm inspired in these
matters."

As we drove home, I sang a few words of "O Christmas

Tree," but Mark turned on the radio like the kids always do when I sing.

I quit singing, turned down the radio and said, "Mark, about this tree."

He looked over at me as I continued in a most serious tone, "When your mother asks how we picked it out, why don't you say, 'We went to 47 different tree lots. We looked at 4,752 trees and finally after comparing each of those we chose this perfect tree.'"

His reply was, "That's not true." When I heard him say that, I found myself almost wishing that he'd not paid so much attention to all the Sunday School and Primary and home evening lessons on honesty.

We got the tree home and Marilyn was pleased. She didn't ask if I'd looked around before buying it. She knows enough about me that she doesn't ask many questions anymore.

She didn't even seem to pay any attention to Mark's indicting statement, "Dad bought the first one he saw." I felt like not getting him his electronic game for Christmas. But that would have deprived me of a lot of fun, so I quickly forgave him.

Marilyn asked, "How much did the tree cost?"

I replied, "I got this wooden stand for nothing. The young man even nailed it on for no charge." I then picked up the tree by its stand, told Mark to grab the pointed end, and we marched triumphantly into the front room.

I turned on some Christmas music, backed off, turned around, crossed the room, and sat down in a soft rocking chair.

My task was over. Now it was time for Marilyn and the four children who were at home to go to work.

The box that contained the ornaments, electric Christmas lights, silver rope, and some used icicles was opened. While I watched from my most relaxed position, the decorating began. I heard words like, "A little higher, a little lower, good, just right." I watched admiringly.

As they worked, I listened to everything from "Rudolph" to "Silent Night." I felt feelings of looking forward, of looking back, of love, and of pride. Laughter and love filled the air. It's hard for me to imagine a room ever being more jam-packed with Christmas.

Finally the last tinseled icicle was hung. Without leaving my chair, I shouted, "Pull the drapes so it will be darker in here. Then plug in those lights and let's have a look."

A few seconds later the only word I could utter was the best adjective of all, "Ahhhhh!" There is something so special about the first look at the year's freshly decorated tree.

A few minutes later we were gathered at our round table for lunch. As I sat there with my family, I wondered if there ever had been a richer man than I. I looked at the food before me on the table. I supposed to myself that only in rich families like ours would each family member have a different-colored drinking glass. Only rich families like ours would have hamburger all mixed in with macaroni.

As we were eating, I asked Marilyn to please pass me the margarine. She replied, "Call it butter."

"I'm too honest," I responded.

Sitting there with my family it was almost as if I could hear a pounding on our window. I knew that if I opened it, I might be knocked off my chair by a current of Christmas blessings coming from God and pouring into my home and into my heart.

About that time my little black dog, whose official name is "Little Dog," seemed to sense my happiness. In his own way he begged me to take him for a walk down the lane that leads along the foot of the mountain.

I was glad to grant Little Dog's wish because that path along the mountain is among my favorite places. It's one of the places where I like to go when I want to be near the source of all joy.

That December day was briskly chilly, but with my coat buttoned tight and my earmuffs in place, I was comfortable. As we walked along, Little Dog would leave my side and dash into the oak brush and around each sage bush. Then he would come back to the path to thank me for bringing him to such a dog paradise.

When I walk, my mind often fills with wonderful thoughts. And this time of year I couldn't seem to think fast enough to include all that clamored to enter my mind.

Soon I was passing in front of the old machinery that had once been used to pull gravel from the mountain.

In about twenty more yards I came to my favorite praying and thinking spot. I stopped and stood very still. Little Dog looked up at me and then darted off to search for grey birds. I turned and faced the steep slope of the rugged Mt. Olympus. Starting at the lower ridges, I slowly lifted my eyes to the top. I love the mountains, for they cause me to look up. Somehow they give a feeling of strength and hope to my life.

Little Dog seemed to understand my need to be alone and he romped higher and higher up the slope.

I turned back and gazed at the great valley. I began to pray. I can't describe all that I said—some with words and some with silent thoughts. I didn't really ask for anything. My main desire was just to thank him who made Christmas.

I recall that as I looked down at all the houses I remembered my brother Kent's words, "How could one man in one night..." I smiled and chuckled to myself. Life had been good to me. I was so glad my mom had been my mom and my dad my dad. I was so glad I had grown up when and where I did. I said softly, "I wouldn't trade places with anyone in all the world." I looked up into the clear blue sky and thanked him for it all.

I remembered the toy gun and the broken ornament. I had promised I would never break another one and I hadn't. There is so little bitterness about past follies when we know we have changed our ways.

In my mind I remembered all the things that can be built with Tinker Toys. I wondered why the directions that showed how to make a thousand things never once mentioned how to make Tinker Toy soup!

I remembered the feelings I had had in England when all of what I had thought Christmas was was taken away, and how that had freed me to find out what Christmas really was. I realized again that following the star was not something to be done only once, but that that journey must be taken over and over again.

There on the base of the mountain I felt I was finding him again.

I remembered again the night I decorated the tree for my dad. I could see how he and Mom looked when they saw the tree. I could hear Dad's voice saying, "George, don't forget the star."

Through the years I've heard much of the spirit of Christmas. There on the mountain I felt every degree of that spirit and my soul vibrated with joy.

Suddenly I felt an urge to hurry home. I wanted to be with my family. It's good to be on the mountain but it's even better to be home.

As we walked along, my neighbor shouted out from his porch, "Merry Christmas."

"Oh, yes," I replied.

I was so glad for Santa Claus and Christmas trees and shopping, baking, and sending cards. All were part of the season. But most of all I was grateful for the sacred time—the Christmas time.

A few minutes later Little Dog and I were home. The tree was up. The star was on top. The gifts were made, the cookies baked. I was ready for Christmas and I was happy.